ALL THE GREAT TERRITORIES

Crab Orchard Series in Poetry
First Book Award

ALL THE GREAT TERRITORIES

MATTHEW WIMBERLEY

Crab Orchard Review &
Southern Illinois University Press
Carbondale

Southern Illinois University Press
www.siupress.com

23 22 21 20   4 3 2 1

Cover illustration: "Winter Sunset at Roan Mountain," cropped. iStock; skisergel.

The Crab Orchard Series in Poetry is a joint publishing venture of Southern Illinois University Press and *Crab Orchard Review*. This series has been made possible by the generous support of the Office of the President of Southern Illinois University and the Office of the Vice Chancellor for Academic Affairs and Provost at Southern Illinois University Carbondale.

Editor of the Crab Orchard Series in Poetry: Jon Tribble
Judge for the 2019 First Book Award: Vandana Khanna

Library of Congress Cataloging-in-Publication Data
Names: Wimberley, Matthew, 1989– author.
Title: All the great territories / Matthew Wimberley.
Description: Carbondale : Crab Orchard Review & Southern Illinois University Press, 2020. | Series: Crab Orchard series in poetry |
Summary: "An elegy to a father, Matthew Wimberley's 'All the Great Territories' explores both the relationship between a child and a parent and the landscape of southern Appalachia" — Provided by publisher.
Identifiers: LCCN 2019026173 (print) | LCCN 2019026174 (ebook) | ISBN 9780809337736 (paperback) | ISBN 9780809337743 (ebook)
Subjects: LCGFT: Poetry.
Classification: LCC PS3623.I5875 A45 2020 (print) | LCC PS3623.I5875 (ebook) | DDC 811/.6—dc23
LC record available at https://lccn.loc.gov/2019026173
LC ebook record available at https://lccn.loc.gov/2019026174

Printed on recycled paper ♻

All goes onward and outward, nothing collapses,
And to die is different from what any one supposed, and luckier.

—Walt Whitman

CONTENTS

*

**

ALL THE GREAT TERRITORIES

*

BLACK MOUNTAINS

This isn't a goodbye.
The sun goes down
in the west to push spring
up through the earth. I've heard
painted trillium have bloomed
in the hills of the desolate world.
The moon tries thirty different ways
a month to move us
closer. Tonight it's not there.
I've loved more than you—
darker, broken things.

HOMILY

Good evening of the Lord.
The gravestones open
out of the dark like stag horns
through the whitetail's skull.
In the Valley of the Cross
the five names of the five
sacred wounds are nailed
into fence posts and black cherry.

Forgive those who trespass
this patch of strawberries
beyond the garden's edge—

those who mistake a turkey feather
for a hawk's. Forgive
the breastfeeding mother
who lifts her shirt, rubs
her ribs and flat stomach,
praising the new muses—
benzodiazepine, methamphetamine.
Her son in her hands,

a rotted apple eaten to the seeds. Bless
his unwashed neck and knotted hair,
his shoulder blades piercing toward heaven.

Taking the long way home
I'm thinking of the faces
I've seen, appearing
around each bend, staring out
over the spears of goldenrod.

ELEGY WRITTEN IN DUST KICKED UP ALONG A BACK ROAD

after Larry Levis

Maybe grass
gentle against the anklebones
of cows going up and over
the pasture
becomes no different than people
who turn to light
at the end.
One Christmas
a man only a little younger than I am
took off his clothes
and left them piled on the living room floor
like an atoll risen over blue tile.
His mother found them the next morning,
and framed by a window
saw him hanging in the backyard—
an extension cord tied around his neck.
And because she could not undo the knot,
and had to wait an hour for the police
to make the drive through the remnants
of a snowstorm, she went inside
to do his laundry.
Only when officers took down his body
did she begin to cry.
As I walk a fenceless cow pasture
a few years later
grass has lost its green
and fall is coming from the west.
Something about piles of leaves
reminds me of the first girl I loved.
Her hair the final color fall takes
after the veneer of rust has dimmed—
treetops left devastated

as I was one afternoon.
The air sweetens in the decay of maple leaves
brittle on the ground, they break apart
like paint flecked off old pottery.
Miles from here a mother is crying
kneeling down beside a headstone.
This time of year, when I'm home
I could say I never left.
In this part of the country
time passes with each football season.
Friday nights when fog raises a white flag
from the end zone
as people park a half mile
from the stadium, their cars like crooked teeth—
I'm reminded that once in high school
a quarterback led the team to the state championship.
And, for three years after, playing second string
at a division three college
returned home after flunking out
to work his father's tree farm
and one day walked barefoot into the snow
to climb a seven-rung ladder,
slip an orange cord over his neck
and step out. This is all true, except
I couldn't tell you
anything about his mother,
how light hushed over his grave.
Can't say how long
it took the police to plow
snowdrifts large enough to swallow a man.
Or if his mother did his laundry,
or what his bruises looked like,
how many steps he had to climb.
Even this field
I couldn't show you on a map.

But ask me about the grass;
the wind through the meadow—
and the drawl of branches after a passing storm.
Or stadium lights turned on
humming through the fog,
the single voice of an entire county
rising through metal bench-seats
as a young man dives into the end zone.

IN THE MORNING, THE SPIRIT BEGINS
TO SPEAK

Even the red shingles chipping and scarred
on the roof of the Kangaroo Express
mattered once. And, the starry aftermath
of insects smashed across the windshield
bright in the foreground of sunlight
and fog. This morning the trees
discuss their custody of the light
while above the crows cry out
like nails cleft from wet wood—
it is all the sound the spirit makes and so
it is easily misheard in the early morning
as wind or the downshift
of a salt-truck miles away. Still,
you go out barefoot into the gravel
and listen. You lean in, but only hear
the living. This morning three boys
show you a fly-eaten dog
they found in the park; half-shaded
by briars. Its brown fur
slack over the bones like linens placed
over the body of a king. Where is
the name for the thing left behind
when its life goes off and becomes memory?

Because you believe the spirit speaks
in a voice no louder than the wing beat
of a moth awake in the darkness,
you know it might be impossible
to hear. This morning you're home.
In a room at the other end of the hall
your mother undresses

touching the horizontal scar on her stomach
where a scalpel cut you into this world—
where the light rushed in like a hawk
and was sewn up, left shining in the blood.

THE SNOW SPEAKS ITS OWN NAME

Here I can descend into the briars
and disappear.
If there is anything to show you
in the ideograms
slipped from the corner of a horse's mouth
like cold spangles of frost-light,
or the way the moon
looks like an upturned keel the color of used chalk,
maybe it's the way the horse's breath
hangs in the frozen air,
unthreading the dark.
Once, in adolescence
driving forty minutes to school
I remember the long line of fire
burning the top of a gorge
and a hawk circling overhead
wings spread in smoke
and the candor the morning sky
made of each feather
patterned like pages. Again
on a Friday night, I walked the quiet street
at the center of town, past the gas station
with two working pumps and overheard
the cashier singing behind the garage door.
If I loved anything then it was a girl I never slept with—
the shade of her freckles
as I lifted her blouse over her head
in the back seat of my car. I won't think
of her fine touch
on my hands as I drove her home a last time
or the way she picked a few daisies
and held them beside her eyes before placing them
in her hair—I won't think of them

in their short goodbyes. Tonight
from this side of the ridge
I can step across the late fallen snow
speaking its own name under
my boots. I walk down the open rows
of a horse stable where nothing moves
except wind buffeting the abandoned flies
wrapped in the torn web
of a barn spider, adding their pallid blue
to the brown boards, a dull hush
strewn over them—the ringing of summer
and their whorled flight and constant buzzing
locked in darkness now.
Maybe it's all lost—the gravel roads
paved over a mile at a time, the walls
of a church in Foscoe overcome with fire
on the coldest night of the century,
and reduced to cinders
and how alike the ash from the hymnal is
to ash from a child's drawing.
Maybe the child witnessed the shingles
revealing the quick insignias of flame
and stood in the cold air, in disbelief or awe
waiting for the bright sirens to appear.
Now that the embers have cooled
and because it could all go away
and because I feel it on my neck
there is one thing I want to remember
for the rest of my life about wind—
its indifference, how it passes
as a stranger you're unable to follow
and can only admire as it moves between
downed leaves, smoke, the flickering
of an untamed fire.

POSSUM

I stand at a fork in the path
beside a vine of barbed wire
wanting—for only a breath—
to see myself at seven
coming upon this spot
stopping in the same trough of trail,
eyes looking into a scaffold of trees
and finding a possum someone strung up
as a warning in a low branch,
dead and rotting. I remember
how evenly the skin decayed
over the jaw
exposing a wide grin—
the body stretched into sorrow's outline
a broken branch stabbed through
its side. Dust and fur shed
from vertebrae
in summer's flat light—
the color it made of bones,
opaque claws turning turquoise
before being changed altogether
into slivers of smoked glass.
And the naked tail
stiff and furless
became beautiful
a fine lace spun in the wind,
the body untouchable.
Always there would be
something in the bend of that shagbark—
a smile unchanged for months.
I walk ahead until I see my porch light
cast a glow against the fog.
It's almost winter—

frost covers the wooden steps.
Overhead the constellations are recognizable
scaled down across my knuckles.
I can hold them one at a time
on the flat of my hand.

PHENOLOGY

After, awake to a bird call
somewhere in the uncountable
trees, I watch the haze burn up
the mountainside from behind
a still-dark ridge until the sky
resembles the worn black metal
of a Thomas arc welder.
I go inside and turn down
the news. All around, the wild
calls out. I hear it now,
the way it persists. I want
to go back ten years
and see how it began to vanish,
a new road,
a Kubota tractor abandoned
in a field cleared for somebody's
second home—the woods
pushed back and back and back.
This is the progress
we read about in books—
Mr. Pucket explaining our history
to us in the seventh grade
when I would stare
out the window
and erase the world with
the haze of my breath.

Most days, driving miles
up from town,
I can feel it beginning
to go wrong. The wish
come true as it tears
apart the dandelion. Time

works her saw blade
across the land—each road
a kerf mark, each Dollar General
a burn. I'm a scientist
recalling an extinct thing
the carbon of it unchanged.
I want to catalogue each new snow,
each titmouse perched in a shagbark,
and the bear cubs grazing blueberries
into the day, the stars, delirious in spin
toward the horizon. If it won't
last, is it enough to watch
each rough bloom? To listen?
A bird is crying out. I hear it.

HUSK

It's been two weeks
since I've seen any stars
just the electric lights
of Manhattan blurred
on the East River's surface.
I rode back to Brooklyn,
the midnight train a cage
speeding below noisy streets—
away from drunks stumbling
down 2nd Avenue; the broken-arm
prostitute on a corner in Alphabet City
who swings her pocketbook
with her good hand—then tries
to hide her face under
wild hair in the breeze
as it brushes her skin.
In the subway car
I stood against a window for half an hour
lightly gripping a chrome bar,
cool air from the vents—
spun dust from a gravel road
traveled by a lone truck. My other hand
held a book as if carrying
some partly living thing.
Reading a book
is a lot like skinning an animal.
Ink has a scent,
a sulfur smell of life eked out.
Here is how it's done, as it's been done
by those who came before me—
no mercy shown, just a calm
blade thrust into fur and bone. Once,
in the foothills of North Carolina

I witnessed a man easily sink his knife
between the match-thin ribs
of a rabbit—peel back skin and place
gallbladder, heart, and liver
in an ice bucket, then heave
what was left into a ditch.
The steaming flesh
cooled in its blood. Earlier,
he'd killed a horse on a blind curve,
brought it home and placed the body
on a hook outside the shed
so it would dry out in the sun.
I remember him showing me his tools
the hose used to wash mud from boots—
the rusted hook where the horse would be
gutted and then made into leather. Years on,
the boards were still stained almost like paint,
like a shadow, where blood soaked in.
When the day was done, we loaded up his truck
and drove away from the rabbit's husk,
now something no longer animal,
eyes left open to catch whatever starlight
spilled through.

ON TRIAL IN THE COURT OF NATURE

Then, you try to confess your crime
of turning the world into words
to the mosquitoes flickering in the dark—
"Don't be an idiot" they interrupt,
shuffling their wings against your face.
"If I may address the court," you ask the flies
bobbing in a glass of milk
but they say nothing, like gods.
The whippoorwill will sentence you
to stand for nights on end in the forest
and examine every stone, count the bronze
beech leaves, every burl, the petals of chicory,
the rattlesnake master, the thunderstorm
passing overhead, each seam of lightning
breaking the sky. You object to the witness
of sunup and sundown. You begin
to think it will take your entire life,
and you grow thirsty and open your mouth
trying to drink the rain.

TO A STRANGER LOST IN THE COUNTRY

To go back,
you will follow
along the plank fence
where the three horses grazing
the silver grass a half mile
from town will stand all night
and listen for the moment
their hooves become sleep.
Below them
the road winds into town
and the shadows
of clouds precede you
like hearses
over everything
and you are empty
and so wish to be like them
little by little.
Beside the crossroads
in a Circle K parking lot
your lips crack in the cold
as you pump 87 unleaded
into your truck,
breathing in
the vapors of gasoline
from the nozzle
and filling a pot hole—
iridescent and smooth
like the skin
of an extinct bird
in a museum—
beautiful, ignored.
You shove your hands
in your pockets,

watching the salt truck
pass ahead of the first ice
and inhale the winter:
diesel exhaust of school buses
and poplar smoke.
Again you see the cashier
mopping the grease
off the floor underneath
the spinning hot dog tray
and notice how she
turns her head
as if searching her reflection
in the tin metal
for some sickness
which will be her end
and she could be dancing
if there were music
and not the crunch of gravel,
and the thud of fuel thick in the line.
You had to come back
and see how it's changed
by staying the same
like sunlight
on the brown surface of a pond.
To see clear—
even as the fog thickens
before you—
you'll have to go inside
and stare back at her
and become her
in the dull fluorescence
of the store. Don't ask me why.
Suddenly your hands will feel thin
and the bra wire
worked out of the fabric

will cut at your skin
and you'll taste the dry lipstick
smeared at one corner of your mouth.
Then, you'll watch
a stranger get into the truck
and disappear
as you kneel over the bucket
of mop water
as if for a moment you remembered
a life you left behind and it presses
against your temples
and then you feel the sharpness
in your stomach
and hear the lice
clicking in your hair
and then like that stranger
the feeling is gone
and outside nothing moves.
Your life drifts by you. You stock the aisles
then hunch over the register
waiting for the early hours
to worry loose the mountains
from the sky. You take the cash
handed across the counter
and go home with ink and silver foil
caught under your nails.
As for me? I left
it all behind and planned
on keeping my distance—
like a junkie trying to stay clean.
But curiosity of what might be spun
around me like the nests
of webworms
and so I come back
as a witness and to live.

You might see me
down the road, a little sleep
caught in my eyes,
smaller and tired still gazing
at the horses rehearsing
their blessings to the ageless
meadow and I will catch
your stare and let you
become me the way
light becomes the laurel
and you will take your time
and at last be home.

*   *

PRELUDE

The night before the funeral
I carve his face out of the dark
with an outstretched finger
scraping the wreckage of dusk
on the window glass and over
the hunched frame of a storm-
ruined hay barn.

It's 2012, the year the world ends.
The grackles widen over hornbeam
like notes on sheet music
at the far edge of the land. Once,

my mother took me
away from my father
below the quarter moon.
She drove a '76 Gremlin,
ready to be junked and forgotten
by the time I was born.
There is no need

to go back. To watch the sunrise
in the side view mirror
like the bright painted steel
of a Ferris wheel in a traveling fair.
There's a night that sleeps
and a sky for darkness and for burial,
for ash, and flight.

ALL THE GREAT TERRITORIES

"And see the land, what it is;"
—Numbers 13:18 KJV

This dust whorled out of drainage ditches,
this snowbound field in February
the broken barbed-wire fence
and the sun climbing over morning
to trespass into the western sky.
This town so small you can see
where it empties on the surface of the millpond,
the bells from the Baptist church
calling to arms the white bodies, bruised
and covered in inconsolable shades
of paint and roofing-tar,
so they might hear the angels and good news.
This county with no bookstore
and the methadone clinic like a hornet's nest,
the men and women in line as if preparing
to accept their Savior. This high school
where one of the slow girls
knocked up by her mom's boyfriend
wets herself and spends a day
in damp overalls rocking in her own arms.
This football field—its hundred-foot lights
and AstroTurf. The collision of bodies, the rain
beating on helmets, the stench of jerseys,
the gay teenager cheering over the boos
and threats of dismemberment and—
months after being disowned
—his cry as others hold him under the bleachers,
breaking his femur with a sledgehammer.
The way he held his tongue and wouldn't speak
a single name but knew each letter,

flattened them out and sewed them
into his scars. This fine thread of cruelty,
its blue line left in the flesh for good.
Him, spending a year relearning
to walk, learning to repent for his sin.
And those boys whose hands
pressed deep into his skin
still nameless, covered—here, also
where anything is possible.
This morning of valley mist,
and the last cedar waxwing lifting into the sky
as a police officer pulls six Mexican painters
out of a van, spitting at them: *On your knees.*
He's smiling into his radio, no one speaks,
one man whistles in his son's ear.

This same road, this double-yellow line
winding between mountain pastures
and trailers with the Stars and Bars
stretched out from the sheet-metal siding,
passing baptisms
between ice-floats in the Elk River, the Flick Video,
the tanning salons, and Salvation Army.
This road—crumbling into shadow,
nothing else as American—
passing the Whiteway Grill, into Tennessee
under the blade of moon slicing the blue
at midafternoon, as the world begins to level,
spread out on the hood of an SUV. This engine
with 300,000 miles, with rusted chrome fenders,
a broken grill. This trunk filled with supplies
enough to last two months. This bottle of brake fluid,
this sleeping bag, this cook pot, this lantern,
this can of black beans, this canteen,
this shovel. This velvet bag, this gold embroidery.

Unopened. To look inside would be
to look back as if looking across a clear night,
cold, stripped of clouds—and inside, gray powder,
once bone and blood, once able to climb, and run,
once every word ever spoken. Fifty-eight years,
the memory of divorce and living alone—
of three packs a day, and auto auctions.
Once a beating heart, half a pound.
This life siphoned to dust.

*

This is the first time I've opened a Bible in years.
My father's business card slid into the Old Testament,
ready to sell a used Camry to a shepherd.
I can see his white hair slicked back, the glint
of his teeth, the gap where one fell out.
It looked like a door kicked in by a thief
who wanted to ransack the bloodstream.
The last time I saw him: Christmas morning,
half naked and asleep. To really go back
is to begin after the funeral, with this scent:
swamp-flowers on a warm road, the Atchafalaya Basin
slicked green, moss bowing to touch the water. And rain,
bringing traffic to a stop for an hour—the brake lights
glowing like distant campfires before the world
was divided into lines.
A million years of tectonic shuffling
and erosion in each grind and thump.
My father was with me, bodiless
passing the bluebonnets going up
over the hills filling a blank sky, and in the desert
of southern New Mexico, Roswell lit up like bones
on an X-ray after sundown. In the Great Sand Dunes
a hawk's wings spreads thunderclouds
over the snowcaps like the cloak

of a stonemason who slowly chisels
rock like the wind. This wind,
blowing wildfires toward Denver,
has come out of the past life to be felt
like stinging nettle and pebbles
poking into boot soles.

*

In this country, snow melts in the hoof prints
of an appaloosa grazing the Great Divide—
the blood flowers begin to rise out of loam.
This is how I remember
crossing the border into Canada:
the ashes undisturbed for 2000 miles under
an olive-colored blanket and jumper cables.
This is how I left America. The border agent asking
if I had weapons of mass destruction, child porn,
bananas, or meth—pausing to lift one bag and examine it
as one counts toes on an infant. When I tell him
he's holding my father he tucks the sack back into the trunk
and waves me into a stand of pines—
the sun tending a brushfire on the horizon.
This is a letter written in exile
from my father, one his mother asked me to write
years earlier. This is all to show him something
he didn't intend to see. My father
turned away from me and headed out
years before his end.

*

It's four in the afternoon
and this road begins to carry me back
into the Blue Ridge toward home.
This is where I first wanted to let go of everything
handed down to me in legal documents meaning

I owned my father the way a god owns a universe,
like birdseed to be pecked at and carried
into the forest. This last breath taken, Marlboro smoke
whipping past his lips—his bruised face—black scythes
swept above his cheekbones where his face
broke on the floor, and the last sounds
his heart made—this, loud enough to destroy time.

INCINERATION

1.

Because it's my memory I can give it to you—the stars
        and the pine trees, their charred trunks
with blackened limbs and pockets of sap, the scent
        of cold earth
and my father still breathing, smoke covering his lips.
        And the worn motel, someone
with a deck of cards—even a deer and a palomino who don't move
        when you shine a light toward them,
unable to notice how their open eyes become dahlias and then,
        another imitation of darkness.
There on a folding table is a stale piece of Wonder Bread
        resting on a Dixie plate—only it looks
more like a man curled into himself as if he wanted to crawl
        back into the womb.

But it is only bread. If I'd taken a bite it would taste
        like open air.

2.

While at the gas station, a van drives up
        to the cash-operated pumps
and the language of migrants is quiet laughter
        and wind. You can hear
how it's working, over the guzzle of a gas tank,
        how it means the lifting of wrists
and three dollars an hour. But when one of them
        looks over at me, what he cannot see

is how his face does not belong to him,
            as smoke rolls across it,
but becomes my father's, vanished
            from this world.

3.

            I thought if I didn't move, maybe it would last,
maybe outside stars would come out, and the spiders
            would build one final web
I could stay inside.

He looked unreal, made-up into a poor imitation—
            hair cut short and face shaved into the style
of eternity.
            Because of the symmetry of his body
I reached down and stroked the lapel,
            kissed his forehead,

            and, I don't know why I did this,
opened his eyes. And they remained
            in one long gaze of this world as I walked away—
which meant forever,

            tasting the bitter powder of makeup
hours after I'd left the room and his body slid into a furnace
            to be destroyed and become oblivion.

Now I see his eyes, open as the short crescendo of flame
            breaks over his body—all he had at the end—

moving through him.

HOLDING MY FATHER

When I take what remains of you
into the cool night
I do it with two hands
so it seems I am holding
something else—a stillborn
fawn carried toward emptiness
under a black sky.
My eyes dismantle the dark—
the trees from the hillside,
the salt-rusted truck
from the overgrown grasses
and late wildflowers
still believing in summer.
Opening my mouth
I hear the stars cry.
I forget the mechanics of my arms,
the motion of freeing the ashes
which could become any shape
the wind commands. Slowly
I wander the heart's wilderness
on cut feet. Here, kneeling
I touch the tangles of earth snow will erase,
touch the nothing of you
entrusted to me.

WORDS FOR MY FATHER FROM SALMON, IDAHO

I look at a crumpled napkin
next to my coffee cup on the table
and think its outline resembles
Grand Teton and how I spilled milk
on the wooden surface exactly
where Jenny Lake is. I've mapped
out the last two hundred miles
over the pass from Jackson
in grains of coarse salt.
Outside sun pours over treetops
and is bounced back skyward
by a foot of new snow. It can't
be more than twenty degrees—
the world smells brand new and crisp
the way an axe cuts into firewood.
I brushed against
a fir tree in the parking lot
and now my jacket has the scent
of sap and melted ice. It's been less
than twelve hours since I almost
killed a moose on a road which
corkscrewed around blind curves
and I'm still shaken up. I watched
the moon from the middle of nowhere
and thought if you were here
what would you be doing? The ashtray
on the table would be filled by now
and you'd flirt with the waitress
dishing out scrambled eggs and bacon
all morning to truck drivers and other
men like us who have taken
the life of an animal.

PANTOUM HOLDING AN EXTINCT BIRD

I have touched the last proof of a concept—
Ivory-billed woodpecker, specimen in a drawer.
My father, slag-ash, carbon, rising
through the air like a fury of wings.

Ivory-billed woodpecker, specimen in a drawer,
diminishes into an old light
through the air like a fury of wings.
The silence one horizon tells another

diminishes into an old light.
It is early, the mountain insouciant—
the silence one horizon tells another,
a taciturn boy standing over a body.

It is early, the mountain insouciant.
I touch the last proof of a concept—
a taciturn boy standing over a body,
my father—slag-ash, carbon, rising.

EPITAPH

In the middle of a city I was visiting
I found a garden where someone
strung up from a low oak branch
a painted blue birdcage, circular
and metal, with a little carved angel
suspended on a clear wire and playing
a flute glued to his lips. Behind me a few cars
sighed over sunbaked asphalt. I'd look away
from the angel's face and back, and each time
it would change a little until my father
stared out from the bars.

*

I keep going back to the funeral home:
the polished floors, decorative bouquets
of delphiniums, white roses,
and snapdragons. The old furniture
no one rests in, and the stench
of bleach and piss on the bathroom tile.
I go back to the room where my father
is on display. I remember waiting beside him
for someone to speak up,
say *it's time to go.* I remember
the sound of footsteps in the hallway
like ice beginning to thaw and crack
on the surface of a river. And then, a pause
on the other side of the door
which lasted, and lasted.

*

When I left I know he was lifted
from the casket and undressed—
two hands working across the cold

like ice skaters performing for no one.
The back and forth of hands
preparing the body to be erased.
One pulls the placket of the white shirt
flat, the other slips each button free
knuckles shivering down the stomach.

*

The man who operates the incinerator
eats a mustard and ham sandwich
on white bread every day.
Working alone, no one is there
to question his command of the fire.
He knows a child's ashes from an adult's
and gets paid the same for both.
He knows the room where the body
is burned is called a Retort. In Latin
it means twisted, cast back.
For years, he believed the room
was a place bodies were taken
to give a final answer for life—
the crack and pop of skin splitting
away from bone like cellophane
—heat opening the mouths
of the dead.

*

Father, now you're a child
angel floating in a blue birdcage.
Who told you to play that music
no one can hear anyway? Who cast you
back in wood and metallic paint
and left you here for me to find
years after you were shaped
into darkness? If I turn

and leave you to burn
will you show up again
as a bracelet of light
on my arms one morning
coming through the slanted blinds—
and before that ash
and before that the field
of space? Or, will you appear
as the spider web's symmetry
between two rungs
of a worn painter's ladder? The crow's
forked footprint in new snow?

INFINITY ON THE GLASS

—for Darrell

Out there, beyond the sleeping
rows of shagbark
the fog in the valley is as speechless
as the ice locking the waterwheel
in place. Birdless sky—
there is an emptiness to it all
like the hunters in Brueghel's painting
watching skaters on a frozen lake
make figure eights with dulling blades.
I think of the glass eyes of angels
dark in the stone church
where my father is a smudge of ash
across my forehead. The snow falls
behind them. I have my father's
eyes and my mother's voice—his
truculence and her quiet.
When I come back, as I have to,
to the little town empty-handed—
no one notices. The addicts
smoke cigarettes at the corner gas station
waiting for their dealer
to drive up in a busted Subaru wagon
and sell them some glass. The snow
keeps falling. Oblivious, lost in its pattern.
What happens when the last flake floats
out of the trees? What's left
to make a blankness I can drag
my pen through? In the church
the pastor places his thumb on my forehead
and says suffering can be a condition
for forgiveness. Someone
told me my father did not suffer. In the end,

death was instant. But nothing in his life
was instant. Once, at a café where we could sit
at a window and look out on the wet road
a friend explained infinity to me. He put
his lips close to the window and breathed
until he'd made a gray film on the glass.
With his index finger he cut
a line across it, with two vertical strokes
at each end where he drew the numbers
"0" and "1" then asked "What is this?"
I said "The distance between zero and one."
"And," he lifted his hand "what is half of this?"
again and again until I could see out past it—
to the snow galloping through itself
like laughter that could go on forever.

EMBLEM FOR DEATH CARVED INTO A TREE

I remember a few leaves in the river—
running along beside them
in what seems now to have lasted
an entire summer—
and the river's simplicity,
swirling the leaves.
I lived on a gravel road
with miles of forest out beyond
my bedroom window. The dogs
slept all day in the middle of the road
and no one bothered them.
Tonight, I ask the cold water
if it remembers me
but it keeps changing
and the trees reflect on the surface
more bare than the day before.
Years pass. Always
the leaves come back
as if sentenced to watch
over everything: the whips
of blackberry thorns,
the firework stand across the state line,
oil draining into a pan
carried off by the mechanic
with a cleft lip—and also,
the swearing-in of chainsaws
at the start of the workday
and the voices of twelve people,
men, women, children,
living together in a trailer home
rusting into thin pieces
of nothingness. It took twenty-two years
to hear the suffering in the deep green

return of leaves, in the wish
to go away for good, to be wind
or the stone-made rapids.
My father had to die and become final
for me to think like this. I go on living
by the river alone. I talk for months
to the black willow I know
will outlive us all: me and the koi
in a man-made pond
where the leaves fall into the water
underneath the old stars
sometimes called dead of night.
Right there, I fall in love
with death. I go out of the night
and begin to see it everywhere—
in the yellow and blue can
of acetone, the cottonmouth
bathing on the far shore, the shed skin
of sunlight flecked away,
and in the faces covered in blood
playing over and over
all night on TV. And I think
of the time I spent
talking to the trees
and the river. To the heart shape
I carved into the willow
and then my initials and then
the symbol for death
which had been there
years earlier whorled in the water.

COLD LIGHT

Father, this ridge with steep shelves
of milkweed and thistle
I bring you back to
to watch the buckskins
graze on the hillside—swishing
their tails, conducting silence.
It's taken my whole life
to bring you here
and I can feel each whip of grass
on my legs, smell the damp soil
and bitter leaf rot. The lightning bugs
are out for the first time—
they appear like cinders
brushed back into the air.
I imagine crushing them into powder
as Caravaggio did to excite the canvas,
the pulp of their abdomens
luciferin and luciferase rubbed
across the blank surface. I think
he understood the source of brightness,
even if he had to pulverize elytra
and compound eyes to find it,
to shape shadow and oil
into the face of Christ—the body of God
half-lowered onto a stone table,
one hand touching his wounded side
touching the seam the spirit slipped from.
On a day like this I could give you up
with no one watching,
with dignity. I have always wanted
to believe in an afterlife. Though
there is an after life I've seen
without you. The snows melted,

trillium bloomed, horses unstabled
and left to roam.
It took part of a morning to clean
your apartment, take out the furniture,
bag the clothes, box the silverware
and plates. When it was empty
with no evidence you'd lived
inside, I stood by the window and looked out
over a parking lot and admired
the cut chain-link fence
and overgrown weeds pushing
up through the concrete. Because
no one told me where they found you,
I picked a spot behind the couch,
dropped to my knees and stretched out
on the cold linoleum and imagined the end.
Did you hear the argument
of strangers outside, or the whir
of passing cars? Was there something
worth saying you whispered to yourself?
I pressed my ear into the floor and listened hard
for the lightest scratch of your voice.
When the stars go into their hiding,
buried somewhere as if pressed
into a bucket of thistle-seed
I clutch the velvet bag of your ashes.
The cloth slides against what had been you.
The untouched slag—
half of me—half of every
cell, bone, and blood,
half of my heart.

*

*   *

AT NIGHT

Awake, alone—
broke down on a highway one hundred miles
west of Laramie. Shadows bend snow fences
over hills toward the end of America,
past wheatgrass braided like rope
two feet high and falling in one long tide
as the wind sweeps clear of the trees.

Suppose I can say anything
to him now—infinite
unchained from life.
In the liminal dash glow,
he's out there just beyond
ready to disappear.

My favorite picture of him
is a mug shot. There was a night
when my parents were in love
before I was conceived
and the slow drift between them
wasn't noticeable—he'd knocked a man out,
broken his nose. In the picture he's young
wearing a rugby shirt, back against cinderblocks.
He's laughing, the way a grin
cuts at his cheeks. And his shadow
permanent on the wall,
dark enough to fall asleep in.

SILENT WOODS

The metal can is quiet now, full enough
with ashes like the moon over crossroads
    where the small towns are an afterthought
beside the highway. Some cinder floats up,
escaping orbit, the last rubble left over
    from creation. There,

the upturned bodies of moths decorate
the windowsills like cases of instruments
    closed for good. Quiet now.
All along, the night kept watch over your shoulders
—the field lasted and outlasted hoof and hurricane,
    the crouched hunters

making targets of beating hearts. See
how the snow upholsters the trees
    in the morning where more ash
flickers upward to finish the blueprints
of constellations—the eye of a bull,
    the webbed swan's foot.

Can't you hear the screen door tapping
its loneliness? Or, the loose dog
    chain squawking in front of a singlewide
where a man looks on and becomes a detail—
part of the background—dressed in worn
    Carharts and a grease-stained

Dale Earnhardt hat. Imagine him standing there,
always taciturn watching the snow and the exhaust
    from the rock-quarry machinery
erase the earth. Imagine him long enough
and you'll have to go and see what's behind
    the blank guesswork

of crushed stones, standing in the cold
while your feet go numb, until the air
        feels like knives whipping
past your face in a carnival sideshow—
the thrower blindfolded, unshaved,
        sipping from a Listerine bottle

buried inside his jacket. That air is a new country
just beyond your skin. The thin hairs on the backs
        of your hands are slash marks etched
to keep track of time, and your bright scars,
with you always, are the bars on the doors of eternity.
        Quiet now. For as long as you can remember

you've loved the hour just before darkness.
The washed sky, the shine of taillights
        disappearing around a bend.
You've been out there, walked until your lungs
ached like a footstep in an empty room.
        Because someone must clean

the woodstove, you've been taking your time
and looking out into what's left of today.
        It doesn't even matter.
The cars going by, the waitress across the street
refilling an off-white salt shaker in the diner,
        the slow boy riding his bike through slush

at the heart of town. Nothing complex. Not
the internal combustion engine, heart surgery,
        politics, or money. Not the skull of a deer
overgrown with moss and trillium, or the streams
following gravity down from the mountains. It can all turn
        to ash. Even skin and blood

are accelerant. Most of what I know of living:
the simple work with a maul, the heave of metal
        into poplar, the lifting of wood,
the strike of a match, and the fire curling, the bark
quiet now. Quiet now. There is the word
        you were looking for all along

smoldering in your mouth, burning your tongue
until you open it and say *goodbye.*

GHAZAL RETURNING FROM EXILE BY THE
LIGHT OF A COUNTY FAIR

His grave is a mile from here and I haven't returned—
dusk gathers in branches of black willow, in the tide of the James
        River, returning

as the wild decorations of cardinal flower sewn along the bank
        like embers swept
throughout the marsh without smoke, smelling like powder in
        old photographs, or returning

as the flight feathers of blue jays, the drum of their wings
in the silver limbs of hornbeam. Red light threads the horizon,
        like the return

of a shuttle down a loom, pulling the dyed fabric into a pattern
looking like the far cast shape of a heaven returning

to this world for a few nights as a traveling county fair—the bulb
        lights flickering
on the passing faces of teenagers who smoke cigarettes on the
        Ferris wheel, as it returns

from the sky, the sway of each gondola overlooking the tent tops
        and crowds
coming and going with cotton candy or popcorn, the bumper car
        operator returning

from a trailer with pink ticket stubs falling out of his pockets and
        grease tracked on his shirt
and he looks alive, though you never see him again, and the
        teenagers return

to their parents' homes in the trailer park where they can get
        meth
or oxycodone, and for them their empty rooms become a
        different heaven. Return

if you wake up, to the fairgrounds, now an empty lot. I'll put it
        here on this page
for you to walk up—the footpaths, returning

to the emptiness in the hoofprints of the blue ribbon donkey,
        pressed in the mud,
the tattered fibers of tent canopies left behind—nothing is meant
        as representation. Return

to the row of hornbeam, the inflorescences of jewelweed
        stemmed from a creek
where last night you could have listened to the grunting pigs, the
        returning

cold of late October—when you never have enough tickets to ride
        the Gravitron.
And I've been in my room at a desk, writing about what has
        returned

from exile, and if exile turns away at birth and reenters this
        world
in the form of ash hewn from bone. Once, I watched the swirl of
        the fair rides turning

until they became stillness, until I stopped seeing them at all.
        Then it was a single light
in a window of his apartment, him far off and alone. Tonight, he
        returns

and I remain bent over this page, never looking behind me,
        never
hearing his breath—as if he walked out of exile, and returned

shaded in ochre, saying nothing, only watching,
the fast spinning of a carnival ride in his eye.

THOUGH HE IS GONE, I CARRY HIM DOWN
FROM THE MOUNTAIN

I've witnessed one pure stillness—the mountains
as fog ascends their crooked spines
on a dustless staircase of moonlight.
For months, I lived apart
from my wife—I split firewood
and delivered upscale furniture
to vacation homes. I taught children
similes in a school too poor to buy
bleached white paper. Once, one
of them smiled at her description
of a bird—a bruise empurpled
on her cheek shrinking in delight
like a shadow diminished
on the carpet. Her teacher told me
it was always there, though in some
other shape—sometimes yellow,
or red—and all she could do
was inform Social Services, who
would take the child away from home.
There's more backstory to explain
why she doesn't make the call
but it's too sad to hear if, like me,
you want to believe decency
still exists. Then, I kept my father's ashes
on a bookshelf. My two friends in town
were a poet and a Marxist. The poet
sold painkillers for a living. His son
was a magician, fourteen maybe,
who rode a bicycle around
performing illusions and sleight of hand
for anyone willing to watch—for joy alone.
And the Marxist loved the railroad

and would search out forgotten tracks
always overgrown with creeping thistle
and lamb's ear, even in winter. He would
lie on his back trying to feel
the old world—or maybe it was
only to watch the clouds gather
in a storm overhead, or to be alone
near the middle of his life. On the day
I packed my things to return
to my wife, a hailstorm forced me
to pull over in the first mile. Each
white crystal rang out on the metal
until I heard music—opaque hallelujahs,
and then—the blue trumpeting the sky makes
at the start of all leaving. When it was over
I put the truck in drive and eased
off the brake. Crossing Spice Creek
a half-starved horse roped to the side
of a trailer-home scratched a question
into the earth. His hoof was desire—
shaded under an oak which carried
dusk from the horizon. I passed
the makeshift stands advertising
authentic mountain goods: honey,
apples, jams, bundles of locust—
all for sale and for so little money!
A damp fire burned on the other side
of the ridge. Smoke unspooled.
The stars appeared.
I thought mostly I would be forgotten—
blood in the mosquito's belly.
It's true, the same as the rhododendron
which grows only so high up the mountain,
and how the two deer I saw without fail
each morning, golden and wild,

moved like sleeves of sunlight
down the fields. Once, my father
came here to visit on his own. It was years ago.
He stayed at a hotel where I met him
after high school late one afternoon.
I showed him the town—the deserted
glove factory, the closed hospital,
elementary school, the gas station,
the bar, the millpond. The vineyard
was still a Christmas tree farm—failing
and about to go under after six
generations of work. He commented
how empty it felt and how he could
never live here. When I left
at twenty-seven I'd outlived him
one thousand five hundred and thirty three days.
At what mile did all of this come to me
like crying behind an open window?
At what mile did a robin miscalculate
her entire life and turn her wing too late
before colliding with my windshield—red,
and black, and purple? No, not a robin
—a sparrow.

MYTH

His name is swift water, the abandoned reflection
    of the Tredegar Iron Works—the city's evacuation, the last
      fires
        of a failed revolution. I watch on from the shore. The
        sun exhumed
from the horizon—traffic stalled on the bridge. Over the casual
  curses
    of bricklayers repairing the sidewalk at China and Laurel,
      three starlings
        swoop down to peck at trash in the gravel alley
behind my house—and a group of teenagers smoke on the
  corner
    in the first hours of summer vacation. The gate of a chain-
      link fence is open,
        the latch gone, swinging back and forth. If I could hear
the river from my porch, if I could step into its shallows.
    But I cannot hear it. I cannot feel it.
      Inside I call out, as if he's waiting for me, maybe in the
      kitchen
or coming from the bathroom with wet hands. His name sounds
    like Abracadabra in the empty room. What can a name
      mean once it belongs
        to nobody? Once it's engraved on a bronze plaque
        almost as if
by mistake? When you can run your fingers over the surface
    and feel how emptiness is spelled out? Each letter
      like a cave dwelling of a lost people. Someone had to do
      this,
had to cut away metal, making one thing another. Think, now, of
  Odysseus
    —heading home after the war, finding shelter in a cave.
    Then,

think of the Cyclops returning from a shift in the fields,
    herding sheep
and skipping stones into the water, a pack of cigarettes in his coat
    pocket.
        Think of the salvation a name can bring, the trouble.
        Is my father Odysseus, or Polyphemus? Does his name
mean *Nobody*, does it abide? Tomorrow, he'll still be gone
        and tomorrow, and tomorrow. Swift current, stalled traffic,
        reeds bending on the shoreline.

HERE ON EARTH, 1994

One patch of ground begins to green
in the field where the taller weeds
line the far side—pale against the trees
as the black moon's thread-thin edge—
Mars is out, nearer the stars
in its torch glow
and here on Beech Mountain
my stepfather has parked in the middle
of the road and gone out
in the cool spring night with a blanket
to place over a doe's body—
her two hind legs crushed on the gravel.
Already in shock, the flies design a veil
over her face which keeps changing
depending on the shadows
lengthening in the fog-lights. Her one eye
—I can see—
blinks as he approaches
widening under the sway of the blanket,
the frayed edge brushing fur and blood.
My stepfather kneels and rubs her head,
whispering in one flopped open ear
until her groaning becomes
a sound which is not pain at all
and the thick buzz of flies goes down.
I have yet to call him *Dad*,
this man who loves my mother,
and when he waves for me to come closer
I unbuckle my seatbelt and crawl
from the truck without thinking. And,
as he speaks to the deer I know
we take on trust this way—
alive and full of fear.

ABSENCE

Your dead father
has left the dishes for someone else.
His sweat darkens the floorboards
in a way the snow won't
as you track it into
the living room.
You leave Virginia
and go back to the old world
still an outsider. His eyes
follow you and your new life—
like a child watching the shadows
of fish in a frozen lake.

I walk home late
from the bar.
Between the mountains
the stars blue
and the cows kneel
in the dirt
and say nothing
and the trees, dressed
in a low cloud,
look like script
rubbed on a sheaf
of butcher paper.

IN LIEU OF FLOWERS

This is the last poem for my father.
You could say I've been writing it
for years. It's kept close, always
the reflection of my shadow in a dirty
window. I can imagine him now,
as ash and a fading grin,
with a little relief—what fire must feel
as it becomes smoke and then a gray
pall ragged in the distance. There
the mountains are always home—
a sideshow to the outside world
no one pays to see. Still, opinions
run wild in conversation! I've got
a friend there who spends all his money
on hallucinogens and bills, who barely
keeps the electricity on. He can speak
six languages but couldn't find the words
to save his marriage. When I talked to him
earlier his voice had come to rust.
I don't remember what I was doing just before,
but afterward I went out
into the darkest night in five hundred years
and walked down the road—the houses
full of tourists for a few days, white
Christmas lights draped from the roofs
like icicles. It made it brighter
than it should have been, and the light
danced along the surface of the salted streets
beginning to freeze over. I think
if I'm being honest, I've tried to protect
my father for most of his life, and now
I don't think he needs me to. He was an alcoholic
who'd been married twice

before he met my mother. They were in love,
or they loved one another—and so
I know what can come of that. After
the divorce we found ways to hide
parts of ourselves. Once,
when I was twenty-one
I found a sex toy under his pillow.
I was on a trip to Washington to see
a woman I thought I would marry
and I stayed at his place—an apartment
that smelled like Marlboros and Pine-Sol
like any motel off any highway in America.
I remember waking up in the middle of the night
and my hand brushing something
under the pillow, and then I grabbed the thing
and lifted it up into the air and stared
at it wide-eyed in wonder when I realized
what it was. Then I lowered it, and covered it
with the pillow exactly as before
with a tenderness that surprised me
then went back to sleep.
We never spoke about it, and he made me
toast and coffee that morning before I left.
It feels like another life, now that I'm older
and married to a different woman.
Walking along the A-frame houses
so out of style they will last forever, I can see
a family gathered around a dinner table
on vacation in a house they rented
for more than the cleaners make in six months.
There's a Duraflame burning in the fireplace
and two dogs lounge on the furniture
as if positioned for a portrait.
No one sees me walk by
and anyway, I'm a stranger and I can come

and go as I please. When my father died
we made a deal I could ask him anything.
I signed my name for his remains
and the bank took what they wanted
and for years now he keeps talking, even
when I haven't come up with a question.
What's strange is I don't think
I wanted him to suffer, and stranger still
is I'm sure I did. The air is thinner,
though, unlike paper or a second-hand
as it circles on. I look back through the windows
and the mother is collecting plates,
one of the boys lays his head down
on the table.

ELEGY NEAR LITTLE BLACK PINE ROUGH

I will mourn him
alone, as I could not
that February,
or days later at the church
where the used-car salesmen
slouched in the pews
and the pews complained
for lack of emptiness. Weeks
went by and still nothing. Not
from Boone to Llano, Aurora,
threading northwest through the Wind
River Range, and all the way
to the Pacific. Not here. The map
is a coffin I can't bury him in
and so I've kept him from the earth—
undisturbed and cold.
I do not know why. It's evening.
The flies of summer enumerate,
spin through the air and the dead
limbs cracked from last week's
storm hold on.

THE CELEBRATED COLORS OF THE
LOCAL SUNSETS

The day feels as thin
as the letters fading from
half a can of spray paint
a decade ago on the brick wall
of the closed-down
Suder Feed Supply where we used
to skateboard and think
of all the crimes the police
could punish us with
for being poor, and teenagers,
for wearing skin-tight jeans
and growing our hair
like a girl's, for almost anything—
at least it felt like it then.
I can't imagine home
without thinking of the past
and the faintest stir
of indignation. It's beside the point.
Today, I'm revisiting Miłosz
with a pen pressed to the pages
making notes in the margins.
In 1987, in Berkeley,
he is doing the same, and thinking
back on the end of his countries, their
"posthumous existence." Like him
I know a place
I can't return to, and without
much imagination can picture
everything coming apart, one way
or another. When I imagine
how it might go, it is
just like this: I am memorizing

birdcalls and wild
plants which become a blur
at the far edge of my yard,
their Latin names tangled
in my mouth. Didn't I
already show you this?
The country at twilight
and a far-off darkness
of pines, a deep red sky
imagined for this page. What I left out
wasn't meant to be remarkable—
a bruise faded from the surface,
the wounds buried
like overwintered wasps
plotting assassinations
beneath the snow. So let's see
if I can draw it into focus,
like the truant daydreaming in class
suddenly with something to say—
the one end I know complete.
Once, I thanked my father
for the gift of this life,
something he didn't hear.
It was two years before he died
and he was high
on the translucent painkillers
the hospital ordered to keep him
comfortable after surgery.
It was as real as anything
I ever told him. I stood
over him in the hospital bed
and traced the outline of his body
under the gown, the collar and hip bones,
his stomach, his penis, and balls,
numbered the black stars

printed on the cotton and listened
to him breathe, mouth
open, just so, a way
into the hive growing in his chest.
He didn't hear, and then, he couldn't.
In those years, I barely spoke to him
and now not an hour can pass
I don't hear him, now that
what he has to say is always
final, always a last word. And
Miłosz is buried in Kraków
and my father has entered
eternity as ash, and I am
certain what doesn't last
lasts—*Hydrangea quercifolia,*
Hypericum densiflorum,
Solidago rugosa.

ACKNOWLEDGMENTS

I am grateful to the editors of the following journals where these poems first appeared—sometimes under a different title.

The Monongahela Review: Black Mountains
Day One: Homily
Narrative: Elegy Written in Dust Kicked Up along a Back Road
Shenandoah: In the Morning, the Spirit Begins to Speak
The Collagists: The Snow Speaks Its Own Name
Orion: Possum
Puerto Del Sol: Husk
Narrative: On Trial in the Court of Nature
diode: To a Stranger Lost in the Country
Tinderbox Journal: Prelude
The Asheville Poetry Review: All the Great Territories
Pleiades: Incineration
Vinyl: Holding My Father
Narrative: Words for My Father from Salmon, Idaho
diode: Pantoum Holding an Extinct Bird
River Styx: Epitaph
Vinyl: Emblem for Death Carved into a Tree
The Missouri Review (online): Cold Light
The Paris American: At Night
The Raleigh Review: Silent Woods
Meridian: Ghazal Returning from Exile by the Light of a
    County Fair

The Southern Humanities Review: Though He Is Gone, I Carry
  Him Down from the Mountain
Narrative: Here on Earth, 1994
The Swamp: In Lieu of Flowers
Poem-A-Day: The Celebrated Colors of the Local Sunsets

Thanks to Garret Hongo who selected "All the Great Territories"
as the winner of the 2015 William Matthews Prize from the *Asheville
Poetry Review*.

Thanks to Mary Szybist for selecting "Infinity on the Glass" for the
2016 Best New Poets Anthology.

Some of these poems appeared in the chapbook *Snake Mountain
Almanac*, winner of the 2014 Rane Arroyo Chapbook Contest from
Seven Kitchens Press.

Thanks to my family, friends, and teachers who continue to en-
courage and support me, with special thanks to Will Badger, John
Balaban, Shervon Cassim, Leila Chatti, Tyree Daye, Greg Donovan,
Jeannine Erasmus, Mallory Flynn, Jesse Graves, Vievee Francis,
Sierra Golden, Alysia Harris, Scott Huffard, Dana Isokawa, Eliza-
beth Jackson, Michael Joslin, Kevin Keck, Daria-Ann Martineau,
Amy Meng, Kathy Olson, Matthew Olzmann, Michele Poulos, Cat
Richardson, Darrell Shatley, Nicole Sealey, Keri Smith, Monica Sok,
Anders Carlson-Wee, William Wright, Jake Young, and Emily Jung-
min Yoon.

Thanks to my friends in the NYU Creative Writing Program, par-
ticularly my teachers Catherine Barnett, Marie Howe, Yusef Ko-
munyakaa, Deborah Landau, Megan O'Rourke, and Sharon Olds,
who believed.
  I am humbled and grateful to Vandana Khanna for selecting my
book for a series I've read and admired for years.

Special thanks to the entire team at SIU Press for their dedication to this book. Particular gratitude is due to Jon Tribble, Allison Joseph, Wayne Larsen, Kristine Priddy, Judy Verdich, Linda Buhman, Chelsey Harris, and Jennifer Egan.

The earliest poems collected in this book began to take shape in a 1998 Toyota 4Runner as I drove across the continent in late winter of 2012 with Trevor Brown and Ben Jamieson. I am lucky for such companionship.

Continued support from Greg and Corinne Wilson, Andrew Lawrence, and Graham Ford have been invaluable.

I am forever grateful to J. Scott Brownlee, Jacob Dawson, and Javier Zamora. From New York City out into the rest of our lives.

Many of these poems were first read and supported by Amanda McConnon, whose friendship and poetry I am grateful for.

With gratitude to Eduardo C. Corral, who is a friend and teacher.

Thanks to the inimitable Wilton Barnhardt for his seemingly endless kindness and keen eye, and for always encouraging me to write. I'll look forward to the next adventure.

Likewise, this book and this life would not be possible without the care of Dorianne Laux and Joe Millar. These poems go onward and outward because of y'all.

Finally, thank you to my family, who trust and love: the Blanchards, the Hoffmans, the Kings, and the Wimberleys. Most of all, thank you to my wife, Sally, for her immeasurable patience, kindness, and love.

Other Books in the Crab Orchard Series in Poetry